KIDS FAVORITE BIBLE STORIES

CReated by StepheN ElkiNs
IllustRated by Tim O'CoNNoR

www.mywonderkids.com

Table Of Contents

Baby Moses

The Israelites continued to grow in number. Pharaoh passed a cruel law ordering every baby boy born to an Israelite family to be drowned in the Nile River. Now it happened that a baby boy was born to an Israelite family. Fearing Pharaoh's decree, the mother hid the baby for months. But when he began to cry and move about, she had to do something to save him. She decided to make a large basket out of the reeds that grew near the river. She sealed it with sticky tar so it would float.

Then she put the baby in the basket and set it among the reeds along the riverbank. His sister Miriam stood at a distance to watch over the baby. That evening, Pharaoh's daughter went down to the river to bathe. It was then she noticed the strange basket floating among the reeds. "Fetch that basket," she said to her servant girl. When she opened the basket and saw the little baby boy, she loved him.

Miriam came forth and said, "Would you like for me to get an Israelite woman to take care of the baby?" So Miriam ran back to get her mother and told her the things that had happened. "Take care of this baby and bring him back to me when he is older," the princess said. When the child grew older, his mother took him to Pharaoh's palace, back to the princess, and he became her son. The princess named him Moses saying, "I drew him out of the water."

The Burning Bush

One day while Moses was leading his sheep to Horeb, also called "the mountain of God," an angel appeared from within a burning bush. Moses thought it was very strange that this bush, though on fire, did not burn up. Then God spoke to Moses from within the burning bush. "Moses, Moses," he said. "Here I am," Moses answered. "Do not come any closer. Take off your sandals, for the place you are standing is holy ground." When Moses heard this he was afraid to look at God, so he hid his face.

"I have heard the cries and prayers of my people in Egypt. So go now. I am sending you to Pharaoh to free my people and lead them out of Egypt into a good land, a land flowing with milk and honey." But Moses said to God, "Who am I that I should lead the Israelites out of Egypt?" God answered, "I will be with you."

"Who shall I tell them sent me?" Moses asked. God answered, "I AM that I AM. Tell them I AM sent you." Moses asked, "What if they do not believe me? What if they will not listen?" Then God commanded Moses to throw down his staff. Moses obeyed and suddenly the staff became a snake. As Moses took hold of the snake, it turned back into a staff.

Then the Lord spoke to Moses again, "If they do not believe you, take some water from the Nile River and pour it on the ground. It will become blood." But Moses did not want to go and spoke again. "O Lord, I don't speak very well, and my speech is slow. Please send someone else." This angered God and he said, "Your brother Aaron speaks very well. He will go with you. Tell him what to say and he will say it." So Moses and his brother Aaron left for Egypt.

Let My People Go!

Moses and Aaron arrived in Egypt and went to see the Pharaoh. Moses said, "The Lord God of Israel says, 'Let my people go, so that they may celebrate their deliverance and worship me in the desert.'" Pharaoh said to Moses, "I do not believe in your God and I certainly will not obey Him. The slaves are mine and I will not let them go."

Then Pharaoh gave an order to the slave masters. "Do not give the Israelites any more straw for making bricks. Make them gather their own straw for making bricks. Make them gather their own straw after they have finished working. But I want the number of bricks they make each day to be the same." This made their work even harder.

Soon, the Israelites were beaten for falling behind in their work. Moses prayed, "O Lord, why have You brought more trouble upon Your people?" The Lord answered, "Because of my mighty hand, Pharaoh will let my people go. Tell my people that I am Yahweh, the Lord, and I will bring them out of bondage. They will be free and I will lead them to the land I promised Abraham."

13

Then the Lord said to Moses, "Go back to Pharaoh and tell him to let my people go! I will harden his heart so that he will not listen to you. But through it all, I will show Egypt that I am the true and living God. I will bring many hardships on them and soon the Israelites will be free."

Moses and Aaron returned to Pharaoh's palace and proclaimed, "The Lord has said, 'Let my people go.' Obey the Lord!" Then Aaron threw down the staff of Moses before Pharaoh and it became a snake. Pharaoh called for his magicians. When they threw down their staffs, they also became snakes. But they were amazed as Aaron's staff swallowed up theirs. But just as the Lord had said, Pharaoh would not listen.

God brought many unpleasant things upon the Egyptian people because Pharaoh would not obey God. First, Aaron dipped Moses' staff into the Nile River and it turned to blood. All of the fish died and the smell was terrible. No one could drink the water.

Seven days later Moses returned to Pharaoh and said, "The Lord says, 'Let my people go.' If you do not, I will fill the land with frogs. They will be in every house, even in your beds." Pharaoh said, "I will not free the people." So Aaron stretched out his hand with the staff, and there were frogs everywhere. "Moses, pray that these awful frogs go away and I will let the people go," promised Pharaoh. So Moses cried out to God and the frogs went away. But Pharaoh broke his promise and did not let the people go.

"Let my people go!" cried Moses, but Pharaoh would not. So Aaron struck the ground with Moses' staff and gnats began to bite the Egyptians. Then the Lord sent swarms of flies to plague the Egyptians. They covered the entire land of Egypt, but there were no flies swarming near the Israelites. "Moses, pray that these flies go away and I will free the people," promised Pharaoh. Moses asked the Lord to remove the flies, and God answered his prayer. But Pharaoh would not let the people go.

"Let my people go!" cried Moses, but Pharaoh would not. So the Lord sent a terrible disease that caused the horses and donkeys and camels, even the cattle and sheep to die. Then painful boils broke out on the Egyptians and their animals. Then Moses stretched out his staff toward the sky and the Lord sent a terrible storm. There was thunder and lightning and hailstones falling in the fields causing their crops to be beaten down. "Moses!" cried Pharaoh. "We have had enough! I will let the people go. Now pray that this terrible storm may go away." Moses knew Pharaoh would not keep his word, but to show God's power, he prayed and the stormy weather went away.

Then Moses returned to Pharaoh's palace and said, "How long will you refuse to obey the Lord? Let my people go! If you refuse, locusts will cover the ground so it cannot be seen." Pharaoh shouted, "No!" So Moses stretched out his staff and locusts came and covered the ground until it was black. They ate everything growing in the fields and nothing remained. Pharaoh again called for Moses. "I have sinned, forgive me. Now pray to your God to take away these deadly locusts."

Moses prayed to the Lord and soon came a strong wind that carried the locusts into the Red Sea. Not a single locust was left anywhere in Egypt. But Pharaoh would not let the children of Israel go. Then the Lord said, "Stretch out your staff toward the sky so that darkness will cover the land." Moses obeyed. For three days total darkness covered all of Egypt. Moses again said to Pharaoh, "The Lord says, 'Let my people go.'"

But Pharaoh was angry and he would not change his mind. "Get out of my sight, Moses. And don't you ever come back here again!" Then the Lord said to Moses, "I will send one more plague upon Egypt, then Pharaoh will let my people go."

The Passover

The Lord told Moses and Aaron how to prepare for the last plague. "Tell my people that on the tenth day of this month, each household is to select one perfect lamb. Take care of it for four days and then kill the lamb at twilight. Take some of the lamb's blood and smear it on the sides and top of your doorposts. That night, you are to eat the lamb in haste, for it is the Lord's Passover. On that night, the Lord will pass through Egypt. But when I see the lamb's blood on your doorposts, I will pass over you. You are to remember this day forever, and celebrate your freedom."

At midnight the death angel came and all the firstborn in every household in Egypt died, even Pharaoh's son. But no one died in the Israelite homes with the blood smeared over the door. Pharaoh cried to Moses, "Go! Leave as fast as you can before we all die." The Israelites were free at last.

Red Sea Miracle

Six hundred thousand men, plus women and children set off for the Promised Land. To guide Moses and the Israelites, the Lord sent a huge pillar of clouds to follow during the day, and a great pillar of fire as a guiding light by night. As soon as the Israelites left Egypt, Pharaoh's heart was quick to change his mind once again. "What have we done? We must capture the Israelites so they can work for us again."

Pharaoh took six hundred of his fastest chariots and an army of soldiers to capture the Israelites. As Moses reached the shores of the Red Sea, the Israelites saw the army coming. They were terrified! "We will die here in the desert," they cried. Moses shouted, "Stand firm! Do not be afraid. The Lord will fight for you." Then Moses lifted his staff and the seas parted. It was a miracle! The children of Israel walked through the sea with the walls of water all around them.

The Egyptian army followed Moses into the wall of water. But when morning came, the Lord threw the Egyptian army into confusion. The wheels on their chariots broke. When the Israelites reached the other side, Moses stretched out his staff over the Red Sea. The powerful waters crashed down on top of the Egyptian army. They were defeated. Then the people of Israel put their trust in God.

Water From a Rock

The Israelites continued on through the desert of Zin. They found no water there and the people were very thirsty. They complained to Moses. Hearing their complaint, Moses and Aaron fell face down before the Lord and prayed. The lord said, "Take your staff, gather the people together and speak to the rock that is before their eyes. It will pour out water."

Moses took the staff, and as the Lord commanded, he gathered the people in front of the rock. But Moses was very angry and tired of their grumbling and lack of faith. "Will you ever learn that God will provide for us?" he shouted. "You rebels! Must we bring water out of a rock?" Then Moses struck the rock twice with his staff and water gushed out everywhere. The people cheered and all drank freely.

The 10 Commandments

After three months of travel, the group reached Mount Sinai where they made camp. Then Moses went up the mountain where the Lord spoke to him. The Lord said to tell the people of Israel to obey his rules. Then they would be his special people, a holy nation.

Moses returned to the people and told them what God had said. The people agreed to do all the Lord had commanded. The Lord said he would come before the people in a thick cloud. Everyone would hear him speak and always trust Moses. He told Moses to have the people wash and make themselves clean, for in three days he would come down to Mount Sinai.

On the morning of the third day, there was thunder and lightning. Then a thick cloud came over the mountain and a very loud trumpet sounded. Everyone was afraid! Then Moses led the people to meet with God at the foot of the mountain. It was smoking like a furnace and the whole mountain shook. Moses called out and God answered. God called Moses to the top of Mount Sinai and spoke these words, "I am the Lord your God who brought you out of Egypt." Then he gave Moses the Ten Commandments:

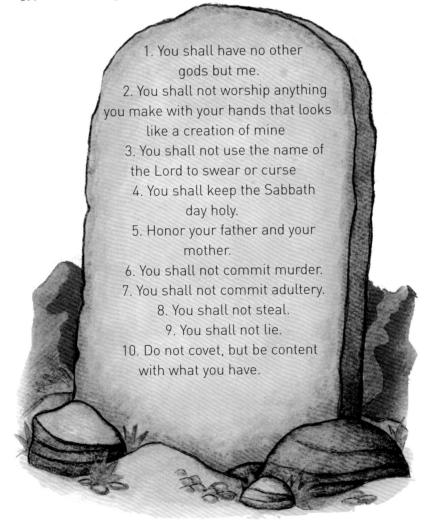

1. You shall have no other gods but me.
2. You shall not worship anything you make with your hands that looks like a creation of mine
3. You shall not use the name of the Lord to swear or curse
4. You shall keep the Sabbath day holy.
5. Honor your father and your mother.
6. You shall not commit murder.
7. You shall not commit adultery.
8. You shall not steal.
9. You shall not lie.
10. Do not covet, but be content with what you have.

Snakes In the Desert

Though the Lord provided their every need, the people continued to complain against God and Moses. The Lord allowed a great number of poisonous snakes to come into their camp. It was frightening and many people were bitten.

The people came to Moses and said, "We have sinned. We spoke against you and the Lord. Pray that the Lord will take away these snakes." So Moses prayed and the Lord said, "Make a snake of bronze and put it on a pole. If anyone is bitten, have them look at the snake on the pole and they will be healed." Moses obeyed the Lord and the people were saved.

Be Holy

The children of Israel traveled through the wilderness for forty years. The lord took care of them, feeding and clothing them all along the way. During this time he taught Moses and the nation of Israel how to worship and obey him. He said, "Be holy, for I am holy." He taught them to bring five special kinds of offerings or gifts to the Lord.

There were burnt offerings given to the Lord to show forgiveness, grain offerings to show honor and respect, and peace offerings, which were animals without any defects presented to the Lord to show thankfulness.